The
Advisory
Book
STUDY GUIDE

ISBN 978-0-938541-14-1
Library of Congress Control Number: 2011932446

Project developers: Linda Crawford, Christopher Hagedorn, and Erin Klug
Cover, book design, and illustrations: Heidi Neilson

All net proceeds from the sale of *The Advisory Book Study Guide* support the work of The Origins Program, a nonprofit educational organization whose mission is to promote an equitable and humane multicultural society through quality education for all.

The Origins Program
3805 Grand Avenue South
Minneapolis, Minnesota 55409

800-543-8715
www.developmentaldesigns.org

15 14 13 12   5 4 3 2

TABLE OF CONTENTS

Meeting Roles and Structure

One of the most effective forms of professional development occurs when educators join together at their own school to discuss a book that can help them develop their practice. When we join a book-study group, we suddenly have more than just a book to read. Now we have to both understand the book and be able to share some of that understanding with others. The extra thrust of shared, interactive learning helps us to read and reflect more deeply and purposefully. Mutual support, interactive analysis, and planning for implementation with peers encourage effective professional development. A well structured book study allows adult learners to do some self-directing, to draw from their own experience, to use their expertise to solve problems, and to gain access to outside expertise, so they are more able and likely to attain their goals.

The *Developmental Designs* teaching approach that underlies *The Advisory Book* identifies productive social interaction as critical to learning for both youth and adults. The approach aligns with research that measures gains in teacher competence from engaging in discourse—interaction that opens up questions and builds understanding. (Tharp, R., & R. Gallimore. 1988. *Rousing minds to life: Teaching, learning, and schooling in a social context.* Cambridge: Cambridge University Press.)

Learning together

In the study group for *The Advisory Book*, you will learn from your colleagues' experiences and their understanding of the text, and they from yours. Listening to others' interpretations, you will gain perspective on your own ideas, as well as a broader, richer body of information about the structure and content of effective advisories. You will build an interconnected community of educators as you exchange analogies, comparisons, inferences, and reactions to the text, and solve the problems that advisories may present to your school or to individuals. Your conversations will help create the context for a successful community-building advisory structure for your school.

Please note that reading assignment and resource page numbers refer to the 2012 revised version of *The Advisory Book*.

Practicing the meeting structures

In the nine meetings of your study together, you will have opportunities to practice components of the Circle of Power and Respect (CPR) and Activity Plus (A+) advisory meeting structures. Having direct experience with daily news messages and trying out a variety of greetings, reflection questions, and discussion formats will bring the structures alive and provide opportunities to identify and resolve problems. Direct experience of the sharing component of CPR is particularly valuable, because you will practice the process of gradually building the elements of good conversation and will be prepared to introduce that process to your students.

The appendices of this guide include descriptions of the discussion and small-group formats that you will be using; *The Advisory Book* provides thorough descriptions of greetings, shares, and reflection questions.

Getting Started

Assignment of roles

The group needs to decide who will do certain jobs for the group. Will one person be designated as the facilitator of all of the sessions, or will the leadership role rotate? Perhaps two participants could share the role. Whether leadership is shared or the role of a single person, someone needs to be responsible for establishing and maintaining the structure of the process.

Schedule of meetings

The nine sessions generally occur in consecutive weeks, but you may choose to extend the process to as much as twelve weeks. Use the schedule grid on page 11 to plan dates and leaders for the meetings.

If you have purchased *The Circle of Power and Respect Advisory Meeting* DVD, it's a good idea to view the recording, or at least the teacher-led meeting (19 minutes), before Meeting One or before you begin to discuss CPR in Meeting Two. Then you will have a visual/auditory experience of middle-level students engaged in a meeting as a basis for discussing the structure of CPR.

It will add to your understanding to watch for the following:

1. Four components: Identify the greeting, sharing, activity, and daily news components.

2. Adolescent needs: Looks for ways that the CPR experience meets adolescents' needs for autonomy, competence, relationship, and fun.

3. Social skills: Look for examples in student behavior of cooperation, assertion, responsibility, empathy, and self-control.

4. Participation: Notice whether all students are actively participating in each of the meeting components.

You may divide into four groups and have each group watch for one of these four aspects of the meeting.

Meeting formats

Sit in a circle for the study sessions. Over the nine sessions, you will experience the CPR and A+ components of greeting, sharing, extended activities, and reflection, and a variety of small-group discussion formats. See pages 66-67 in this *Study Guide* for descriptions of the small-group formats.

PARTICIPANT ROLE

Meeting Preparation

You will use the graphic organizers and questions included in the chapters to interact with the text while you are reading. These tools help you analyze, compare, apply, and evaluate the text in the context of previous reading and your own classroom experience. You will bring the results of your interactions with the text to the next study group meeting.

In addition to the structured interactions, you may also choose to:

- Make notes in the margins or in the Notes space provided about the text or to connect with other ideas and resources

- Underline or highlight particularly salient passages to share with others

- Outline a chapter or section

- Use a set of symbols to indicate reactions, connections, comparisons, and patterns in sections of reading

- Keep a log or journal about the book.

Structured interactions with the text give you signposts to return to when preparing for and participating in the group discussion.

Meeting

Create and follow meeting guidelines

You will participate in creating rules to guide your work as a group. Each meeting begins with a brief check-in on the health of the group and the members' adherence to the guidelines.

Participate in community building

Each meeting presents opportunity to greet one another, share about yourself and your ideas, and participate in discussion activities.

Cite the text

Be ready to cite page numbers and paragraphs to support your text-referenced comments; this allows other participants to see the book's language for themselves. Citing the text strengthens one's case, clarifies ambiguities, and provides context for responses and subsequent conversations.

Listen and respond

After a group member shares his or her thinking, others in the group respond to what has been shared, as opposed to listening without comment and then moving on to the next person's thoughts. Without active responses to ideas, discussions can become dull or perfunctory.

Reflect

The format for reflection varies, but quick formats include:

- **Partner or triad shares:** Two or three participants discuss a memorable element of content of the session.

- **Written reflection:** Participants write comments and questions in the Notes sections provided in their books.

- **Share out:** Several people share with the larger group what they have discussed with a partner or written individually, so the whole group gets to hear some of the individual reflections.

- **Respond visually:** By showing thumbs up, sideways, or down, participants can indicate whether a discussion stimulated new insights, questions, opportunities for commitments, etc. They can also use their bodies to show their responses by standing on or near a "target." Mark the center of the target on the floor with a piece of paper, close to where those with the most positive response stand, and those less certain or less positive responses stand farther away from the center.

Follow up

Follow-up formats are presented at the close of each meeting. Work individually or in groups and report your results at the next meeting.

LEADER ROLE

Meeting Preparation

Successful book study meetings require that everyone read and fully explore the assigned material. The leader can help facilitate this in the following ways.

Review and prepare for meeting format

Read Leader Instructions to understand meeting and discussion formats. Gather materials. Prepare the daily news message. Create a circle of chairs, one for each participant.

Provide reminders

Remind participants of the upcoming meeting dates and times on a regular basis, in a variety of ways, as appropriate: reminders at staff meetings, internal news bulletins, e-mail, the school's intercom system. For the first meeting, communicate the assigned reading to the group at least two weeks in advance.

Meeting

Gather in a circle

Create and post meeting guidelines

In the first meeting, participants review a suggested list of guidelines (see below), narrow them down to three or four, amend as necessary, and approve them, preferably by consensus. For subsequent meetings, post the approved rules.

Suggest meeting guidelines

- Come prepared—read and interact with the text in the manner requested before the meeting.
- Listen carefully.
- Keep an open mind.
- Speak clearly and thoughtfully.
- Participate, but don't dominate or consistently "pass."
- Presume positive intentions in others.
- Only respectful disagreements are welcome.
- Meet your needs, but not at the expense of others.

Guide the meeting format

Gather everyone together at the appointed time and lead the group through the meeting format, the core of which is the small-group discussion.

Meeting format overview

Each study session uses components from the Circle of Power and Respect and Activity Plus advisory structures as well as other strategies to create a rich professional development experience:

- **Daily news:** At each meeting, the leader will provide a daily news message that introduces the session, helps the group gather useful data, and models the use of daily news charts as described in *The Advisory Book*.

- **Introduction of meeting topic:** Specific language is provided in the Leader Instructions.

- **Greeting:** Each session begins with a greeting.

- **Sharing:** Sharing is based on the reading for the session.

- **Small-group discussion:** Chapter discussions take place in the form of an adult learner activity. These are varied from chapter to chapter.

- **Reflecting:** At the conclusion of the small-group discussion, the whole group reassembles to share what was learned.

- **Follow-up and planning:** The whole group considers follow-up activities and the assignment for the next meeting.

Daily news

The daily news imparts information about the session and gathers information from participants; it models ways teachers can use daily news with their students.

Greeting

The greeting process strengthens community and models the greeting structure of CPR and A+ advisory formats. A description of each session's greeting is included here, as well as in *The Advisory Book*.

Sharing

When participants share from their life experiences, they strengthen the adult community and practice teaching the art of conversation to their students. For quality sharing, students need to learn, step by step, how to:

- Select sharing topics

- Speak on a topic

- Ask open-ended questions of the sharer

- Make friendly comments to the sharer

- Try different share formats.

As an alternative to the in-depth exploration of sharing formats provided in this guide, the leader may select sharing formats from *The Advisory Book* and provide a topic for each session.

Guide the small-group discussion format

Lead participants through the small-group discussion format using the detailed description provided for each meeting. Small groups may be formed simply (e.g. Count Off) or playfully (e.g. Screaming Eyes). See the Appendix in this *Study Guide*, for quick ways to form small groups and descriptions of small-group discussion formats used in the meetings.

Guide reflection

At the end of the small-group discussions, there is time for the whole group to assemble and share the thinking of the smaller groups. Participants may reflect on the relevance of what they have discussed to their future practice and perhaps plan implementation.

Guide follow-up reports

Invite participants to report on follow-up work done between meetings, using the format provided for each meeting. When follow-up is a group project, you or a volunteer present the results to the whole group.

Optional

If you have not already viewed *The Circle of Power and Respect Advisory Meeting* DVD, you may choose to view it now or at another opportunity before Meeting Two. Each of the three CPR meetings recorded is about 20 minutes in length (you may choose to show only the first of the three to conserve time). The recorded meetings will provide you with a visual/auditory experience that will clarify your reading and discussion of CPR. At any time in Meetings Two through Six about the four components of CPR you may choose to view a component in the recording again, as a reminder.

Prepare participants for the next meeting

Announce the next meeting date. Direct participants to the next meeting's introduction and Reading Assignment section. Structured interactions with the text are provided for each reading.

Meeting and Leader Schedule

SESSION	DATE	TOPIC	LEADER
1		An Argument for Advisory	
2		CPR: Overview, Daily News, Circling up	
3		CPR: Greeting	
4		CPR: Sharing	
5		CPR: Activity	
6		CPR: Daily News Processing, Student-led CPR	
7		Activity Plus	
8		Planning Advisories	
9		Assessing Social Skill Development	

MEETING ONE

An Argument for Advisory

PARTICIPANT INSTRUCTIONS

Chapter One provides a rationale for teachers to use advisory to create a strong, safe, caring learning community and introduces two advisory structures, the Circle of Power and Respect (CPR) and Activity Plus (A+). These formats for advisory meet adolescent needs for autonomy, competence, relationship, and fun through lively and engaging interaction.

Keep in mind

Advisory refers to a period (sometimes called homeroom) of 15-30 minutes set aside for students and teachers to get to know each other, build social skills, and transition into the learning day. An adult advisor is responsible for each group of advisory students. Ideally, advisory meetings are held in the morning before students begin their classes.

Discussion format at a glance: Affinity Process

In Affinity Process, small groups meet to create a rationale for advisory. Then groups combine to create a larger group, share their rationales, and combine ideas to generate a rationale for the new, larger group. This process of combining groups continues until all participants are in one large group and reach one consolidated rationale.

Reading Assignment

Read Chapter One: An Argument for Advisory, pages 9-28.

Interact with the text: Create a rationale for advisory

Generate a statement of support for using advisory at the middle level. Identify and provide evidence for three reasons a teacher might use advisory. You will share your rationale at the meeting.

Example rationale

Advisory is important because:

1. It meets students' need for relationship with their peers and at least one adult in school. Advisory provides opportunities for young people to greet each other and share about their lives in a lively and fun way. Students are more successful in school when they become connected, feel that they belong, and have strong ties to their peers and teachers.

2. Advisory is important because it provides an explicit, reliable structure for transitioning into a focused learning day. Students play games and laugh with each other and reduce tension.

3. Advisory helps students increase social and academic skills such as engaging in conversation, speaking publicly, cooperating, and playing fairly with others.

Your rationale

1.

2.

3

LEADER INSTRUCTIONS

Meeting Preparation

Familiarize yourself with the Affinity Process format. Decide how many small groups (two to four participants each) you will create. Arrange for an even number of groups, so they can conveniently combine into larger groups during the activity. For example, if you have eight groups of three, the small groups will combine to make four larger groups of six, then combine to make two larger groups of 12, then one group of 24. In this *Study Guide*, see page 15 and the Appendix, page 66, for more on the Affinity Process. Decide if you will show *The Circle of Power and Respect Advisory Meeting* DVD. See suggestion on page 16 below under Prepare for Next Meeting.

Materials: Materials for daily news chart; sticky notes; (optional) *The Circle of Power and Respect Advisory Meeting* DVD and DVD player

Daily news

Prepare and post daily news chart: Direct participants to read and interact with the chart upon entering the room.

Date: _____

Greetings, Friends!

Welcome to the first session of our study group! Today we will discuss Chapter 1 of The Advisory Book and explore the rationale for using this structure with our students.

Do you intentionally do things to build community in your advisory and/or classes? (Make a tally mark)

Never   Rarely   Sometimes   Often   Always

Here we go!

(sign)

Meeting

Gather in a circle

Create goals (5-10 minutes)

Ask participants to write down a goal for their participation in the book study. They can use the Notes space provided at the end of Meeting One. Have each person share his or her goal with someone (this can be done in partners or triads if the group is large). Goals can also be gathered into a chart for group reference. Goals will be revisited at the last meeting.

Example goals

- To learn how to use the Circle of Power and Respect in my classroom

- To have thoughtful conversations about the book

Create rules (5-10 minutes)

Create rules that the group agrees (preferably by consensus) to follow throughout the book study. Suggested rules are on page 8 in this *Study Guide;* the group might use or modify and use them. Post the rules at each meeting.

Introduce topic

Today we will discuss the rationale for implementing Circle of Power and Respect and Activity Plus in our classrooms. We'll consider how classroom communities can benefit from lively and engaging activities and discussions in the meetings. I notice that on the daily news chart...[indicate here the results of the poll on the chart]. We'll start by practicing two community-building CPR components—greeting and sharing.

Guide greeting, sharing, and Affinity Process discussion format

Greeting: Left-Right Greeting (1 minute)

Participants greet the person to their right and left in the circle by saying Good afternoon, _____. Model turning and making eye contact with each other.

Sharing: Sticky Note Share (3 minutes)

Topic: Name a topic that would help group members learn more about each other, for example hobbies, places of travel, or family traditions. Stick the note on the chart.

Each participant writes a sharing topic on a sticky note and places it on the chart provided.

Read each note and tell the group that they will have an opportunity to share about themselves at each meeting using many of these topics. Save this chart for use at subsequent meetings.

Discussion format: Affinity Process (25 minutes)

1. Divide whole group into an even number of smaller groups of up to four people each.

2. In small groups, participants share their rationales for advisory.

3. After everyone shares, the small group articulates three reasons for advisory and writes them down.

4. Pairs of groups combine, repeat the process of sharing, and create a new set of three reasons for advisory.

5. The process of combining groups continues until all participants are in one group. The whole group creates one, consolidated advisory rationale comprised of their reasons.

Reflect: Individual written response (5 minutes)

Ask participants to answer the following questions in the Notes section.

What barriers do you see at your school that may prevent teachers from using the advisory structures of CPR and A+?

What could be done to overcome those barriers?

Prepare for the next meeting

Announce the next meeting date. Direct participants to Meeting Two's introduction and Reading Assignment, pages 18-19 in this *Study Guide*, to prepare for the next meeting.

Optional: If you have not already viewed *The Circle of Power and Respect Advisory Meeting* DVD, you may choose to view it now or at another opportunity before Meeting Two. Each of the three CPR meetings recorded is about 20 minutes in length (you may choose to show only the first of the three to conserve time). The recorded meetings will provide you with a visual/auditory experience that will clarify your reading and discussion of CPR. At any time in Meetings Two through Six about the four components of CPR you may choose to view a component in the recording again, as a reminder.

Follow-up

Discuss and select from these follow-up possibilities. If the group chooses to act collaboratively, designate a leader.

- Gather a team to discuss the current class schedule and identify any barriers to implementing CPR and A+.

- Generate a letter to parents or statement for the student handbook that includes the rationale for advisory. The parent letter could also include explanations of the CPR and A+ formats.

NOTES

The Circle of Power and Respect:
Overview, Daily News, and Circling Up

PARTICIPANT INSTRUCTIONS

The starting sections of Chapter Two provide an overview of the four Circle of Power and Respect components, a close look at daily news preparations and use before meetings, and circling up. Chapter Two is divided into five sections for discussion over Meeting Two through Meeting Six.

Keep in mind

The sequence of the four components of Circle of Power and Respect (CPR) is designed to provide a predictable and productive meeting format. More and less active components are spaced to optimize student attention. The meeting ends not with activity, but with the reading and discussion of the daily news. This closure calms the group after the liveliness of the activity and prepares them to transition into the learning day.

Meeting formats at a glance: Sample CPR and Inside-Outside Circle

CPR: Just as students do, participants read and respond to the daily news upon arrival, then take a seat in the circle. At the designated time, the meeting begins, and everyone participates in a greeting, a share, and an activity.

Inside-Outside Circle: Participants form a circle within a circle, members of each circle facing the members of the other circle. With the person they are facing, members discuss a question about what they have read. After each paired discussion, the inside circle moves clockwise two spaces (the number is arbitrary) to talk with someone else about the same question or about a new question.

Reading Assignment

In Chapter Two, read about the Circle of Power and Respect components (overview), daily news preparations and use before meetings, and circling up, pages 31-48.

Interact with the text

What questions arise when you contemplate using CPR with your students? Write down one or two questions.

As you read about the daily news component of CPR, note daily news questions you might ask your students. Categorize and record your ideas on the chart below.

DAILY NEWS FOCUS	IDEAS FOR DAILY NEWS QUESTIONS
PERSONAL (page 37) Questions that ask students to share information about themselves they are willing to share publicly	
SOCIAL (page 38) Questions that ask students how they behave or respond in a social situation, or about social skills in general	
ACADEMIC REVIEW (page 38) Questions that help students learn or remember content; questions that support learning vocabulary, grammar, or spelling words; questions in any content area	
CURRENT EVENTS (page 38) Questions that prompt students to think about social, political, and ethical issues	

LEADER INSTRUCTIONS

Meeting Preparation

Familiarize yourself with the mini-CPR and Inside-Outside Circle formats. Choose a topic for sharing from the list that the group generated at the first meeting. Determine if you will show *The Circle of Power and Respect Advisory Meeting* DVD during this meeting. See the suggestion on page 21 in this *Study Guide* under Introduce Topic.

Materials: Materials for daily news chart; index cards; sharing-topic chart from first meeting; (optional) *The Circle of Power and Respect Advisory Meeting* DVD and DVD player

Daily news

Prepare and post daily news chart: Direct participants to read and interact with the chart as they enter the room. The poll on this chart will be analyzed and results reported at Meeting Eight.

Date: _____

Hello, Colleagues!

Welcome to Session Two! Today we will begin to discuss the four components of a CPR meeting and think through questions we have about using this format with our students.

How often do you meet in a circle in advisory or during class time? (Make a tally mark)

Never   Rarely   Sometimes   Often   Always

DO NOW: On an index card, write one question you have about using CPR with your students.

For each meeting, we need a volunteer to tabulate responses to the daily news. If you are willing to do this for one meeting, please sign up below. I'm looking forward to our conversation!

(sign)

Data tabulation volunteer(s):

Meeting

Gather in a circle

Post and refer to the rules

Read aloud the group's rules. Encourage active participation.

Follow-up from last meeting (5 minutes)

Ask participants to share their follow-up experiences (see *Guide* page 16).

Introduce topic

Today we will begin to explore the Circle of Power and Respect format and its components. We'll consider the necessary teacher preparations and use a discussion format to address questions we have about this advisory structure. The possible daily news questions you wrote as part of your preparation will help you follow this session by trying out some of those questions with your students.

Optional: View *The Circle of Power and Respect Advisory Meeting* DVD. You may choose to view only the teacher-led meeting portion.

Guide meeting formats: Sample CPR and Inside-Outside Circle

The purpose of this mini-CPR meeting is for participants to experience all the components firsthand. The somatic memory of the experience will reinforce what everyone learns from the book and discussion.

Greeting: Basic (2 minutes)

Leader facilitates a Basic Greeting around the circle. Leader reviews the guidelines for a friendly greeting discussed at the first meeting and models the Basic Greeting format. To demonstrate how to introduce greetings with students, ask for a volunteer to remind the group of the audience's job while others are participating in the greeting.

Sharing: Whip Share (2 minutes)

In a Whip Share, everyone has a chance to quickly share about the designated topic. Choose a topic from the list generated at the first meeting that can be responded to briefly. For example, if one of the topic ideas was "Hobbies," each person can say, *One of my hobbies is _____.*

Activity: Who Remembers? (5 minutes)

Challenge the group to remember what individuals shared by asking questions such as *Who remembers which person in the group likes to swim?* For the hobby theme, ask, *Which people in the group have a hobby that is usually done indoors?* This reinforces attentive listening.

Process daily news (3 minutes)

Ask for a volunteer to read the chart aloud. Direct the group to look back at the interactive question.

This daily news question, like the one from our first session, asks each of us to tell something about ourselves. The responses will enable us to collect a set of data about our group that can be reported back to us. Share with your neighbor the sample daily news questions you wrote in your preparation for this meeting.

Say that each of the daily news charts will ask a different question. On the chart, the leader will ask for a volunteer to take the chart, analyze the data, return the chart to the group at the next meeting, and report significant findings at Meeting Eight of the book study.

Discussion format: Inside-Outside Circle (20 minutes)

1. Ask participants to have ready their index cards from the daily news interaction.

2. Create an Inside-Outside Circle by forming a circle within a circle and pairing up, with partners facing each other (one partner is on the inside circle, the other on the outside ring).

3. Using the questions on the index cards, participants announce questions for pairs to discuss. Allow two to three minutes to discuss each question. If the leader announces the question, s/he should collect the cards ahead of time

4. After each question is discussed, the inside circle moves clockwise a given number of spaces to talk with someone new. Leader designates the number of spaces to move.

5. Process continues with new questions and movement around the circle until you run out of questions or time. Be sure to save time to reflect and prepare for the next meeting.

Reflect: Think-Ink-Share (5 minutes)
What new insights do you have about CPR after our discussion?
Participants think about a response, write it down, and share with a partner and/or whole group.

Prepare for the next meeting
Announce next meeting date. Direct participants to Meeting Three's introduction and Reading Assignment, pages 24-25 in this *Study Guide*, to prepare for the next meeting. Acknowledge the volunteer(s) named on the daily news chart for offering to tabulate the chart data for reporting at Meeting Eight. Remind participants that each meeting chart will ask for a data tabulation volunteer.

Follow-up
Discuss and select from these follow-up possibilities.

• Lead a Whip Share in one of your classes and reflect on the experience with someone in the study group.

• Someone offers to lead a Whip Share at the next staff meeting.

• Try out one or more daily news questions with your students.

NOTES

The Circle of Power and Respect, Greeting

PARTICIPANT INSTRUCTIONS

Chapter Two provides detailed information about the greeting component of the Circle of Power and Respect. The purpose of the greeting is to set a positive tone for the day and to help students learn the skill of greeting others in social encounters. Appendix B is a resource for greetings ranging from simple to complex, low-risk to high-risk, and requiring low to high levels of self-control.

Keep in mind

No one greeting is appropriate for all situations. As teachers gain experience with a variety of greeting formats, they become skilled at choosing the format that best suits the current mood, skills, and interests of their groups. In addition, it is useful for students to learn a variety of greetings, from formal to informal, so they are prepared for the wide variety of social encounters they will experience in life.

Discussion format at a glance: Greeting Sampler

Participants take turns leading different types of CPR greetings. After each greeting, the group evaluates the greeting and discusses adaptations and variations teachers could make in their classrooms.

Reading Assignment

In Chapter Two, read the Greetings section, pages 48-58. Skim Appendix B, pages 217-229, to get ideas for CPR greetings.

Interact with the text

After reading the section in Chapter Two about greetings, plan to lead a greeting at our next meeting. Look through Appendix B, pages 217-229, and choose a greeting that you could lead at the next meeting. Use the planning sheet to help with your preparation.

GREETING PLAN SHEET

Greeting

Activity level

Social challenge level

Is this greeting quick?

LEADER INSTRUCTIONS

Meeting Preparation

Familiarize yourself with the meeting and Greeting Sampler formats. Decide how you will divide into partners and small groups for sharing.

Materials: Materials for daily news chart; sharing topic chart from previous meeting

Daily news

Prepare and post daily news chart: The poll on this chart will be analyzed and results reported at Meeting Eight.

Date: _____

Greetings Friends!

Welcome to the third session of our study group. Today we will continue to discuss CPR and focus on types of greetings we can use in our classes.

Does it matter to you if people greet you by name? (Make a tally mark)

No   Somewhat   Yes   Very much

Best,

(sign)

Data tabulation volunteer(s):

Meeting

Gather in a circle

Post and refer to rules

Ask participants: *How do you think we're doing in following the rules we set up? Do you have any suggestions for how we can get more from our meetings?*

Follow-up from last meeting (5 minutes)

Ask participants to share follow-up experiences (see *Guide* pages 22-23).

Introduce topic

This meeting is an opportunity to learn a variety of greetings for CPR and practice leading a greeting. After each greeting, we'll discuss how and when we would use that format in our classrooms.

Guide greeting, sharing, and Greeting Sampler discussion format

Greeting: 30-second Greeting (1 minute)

Group mingles in the center of the circle or room and everyone greets as many other people as possible in 30 seconds. Leader keeps track of time.

Sharing: Generating questions for sharing (5-10 minutes)

Use the same topic that was used for the Whip Share at last meeting. As a group, generate a list of questions that partners could ask each other to find out more information about the topic. Designate a scribe to record the topic and questions on chart paper for use at the next meeting. For example, if the chosen question is about a favorite hobby, possible additional questions may include:

- *When do you do this hobby?*
- *With whom do you do this?*
- *Where do you _____?*
- *Why do you enjoy_____?*
- *What's challenging and what's easy about_____?*

Tell the group they will have opportunities to ask each other some of these questions at the next few meetings.

Discussion format: Greeting Sampler (30 minutes)

1. Divide into groups of eight or fewer.

2. In each group, participants take turns leading the greetings they prepared. If two or more chose the same greeting, they may lead the greeting together or choose one of them to lead it.

3. Pull sticks to decide the order of the greetings. Depending on the

complexity of the greetings, you may or may not have time for everyone to lead a greeting.

4. Evaluate each greeting after its presentation using the following questions:

When and how would you use this greeting? (e.g. At what time of year would you use it? What skills would you highlight?)

What adaptations might you need to make to use this greeting?

What variations could you try?

Reflect: Individual written response (2 minutes)
Ask participants to answer the following questions in the Notes.

- *What greeting(s) do you plan to use with your students?*

- *When and how will you use them?*

Prepare for the next meeting

Announce next meeting date. Direct participants to Meeting Four's introduction and Reading Assignment, pages 30-31 in this *Study Guide* to prepare for the next meeting. Acknowledge the volunteer(s) named on the daily news chart for offering to tabulate the chart data and report at Meeting Eight.

Follow-up

Discuss and select from these follow-up possibilities.

- Plan to lead a greeting at the next staff meeting.

- Integrate greetings into your advisory and/or use them to begin your class periods.

- Assign students as greeters in the hallway during arrival time.

NOTES

The Circle of Power and Respect, Sharing

PARTICIPANT INSTRUCTIONS

Chapter Two provides detailed information about the sharing component of the Circle of Power and Respect. The purpose of sharing is to help students form positive relationships with each other and develop good dialogue skills that they can transfer to any discussion. Appendix C provides many examples of sharing formats.

Keep in mind

Participating fairly and thoughtfully in a conversation requires dialogue skills including listening, paraphrasing, asking open-ended questions, seeking clarification, disagreeing respectfully, and proposing an alternative viewpoint. Each of these skills must be modeled and continually practiced both during advisory time and throughout the school day in order for students to build their competencies.

Discussion format at a glance: Six Hats Thinking

In groups of six, each person represents a distinct viewpoint, or "hat" (if there are more than six people per group, two people can represent one hat). Each person briefly describes her point of view to the group. The group leader asks questions or reads scenarios, and each person responds from the perspective of his hat. After each perspective has been heard, the group can decide which approach(es) would be best.

Reading Assignment

In Chapter Two, read the Sharing section, pages 59-73. Skim Appendix C, pages 231-234, to get ideas for CPR sharing formats.

Interact with the text: Square, Circle, Triangle

As you read pages 59-73, make notes in the square or circle to indicate how the information you are reading fits with your experiences. If an idea "squares" with your beliefs, record the idea in or near the square. Record questions circling in your mind about sharing in or near the circle. At the end of the reading, record three points to remember about sharing, one at each point of the triangle.

LEADER INSTRUCTIONS

Meeting Preparation

Familiarize yourself with the meeting format, including the greeting, sharing, and Six Hats Thinking formats.

Materials: Materials for daily news chart; sharing topic and question charts from previous meetings

Daily news

Prepare and post daily news chart: The poll on this chart will be analyzed and results reported at Meeting Eight.

Date: _____

Dear Sharers,

Today is the 4th session of our book study. We will discuss the sharing component of CPR and practice asking open-ended questions.

Do you enjoy getting to know people by learning about their lives? (Make a tally mark)

No   Sometimes   Yes

Your study group leader,

(sign)

Data tabulation volunteer(s):

Meeting

Gather in a circle

Post and refer to rules

Incorporate any suggestions for improvement from the previous meeting. Ask participants to identify a rule that's been difficult to follow and brainstorm ways to respect and uphold that rule today.

Follow-up from last meeting (5 minutes)

Ask participants to share follow-up experiences (see *Guide* page 28).

Introduce topic

Today we will focus on sharing in CPR. This component provides opportunities for students to develop the skills necessary to contribute meaningfully to a conversation. One of those skills is the capacity to ask open-ended questions, sometimes referred to as "fat" or "high-quality" questions in The Advisory Book. *Open-ended questions require more than one or two words to answer, and they invite the sharer to respond more expansively. Today, we'll practice asking questions that elicit extended responses —open-ended questions.*

Guide greeting, sharing, and Six Hats Thinking discussion format

Greet: Skip Greeting (2-3 minutes)

Stand in a circle; select a participant to go first. Agree on a number of people along the circle to skip before you greet, and send the greeting around. For example, if you decide to skip two, each greeter greets the third person to the right. After greeting, participants sit. Continue until everyone has been greeted.

Share: Partner Share (10 minutes)

Use the sharing topic and the list of questions created at the previous meeting. Divide into High-Five partnerships. After each partner shares, the other asks two questions to gain more information.

After sharing, the whole group revisits the list of questions and categorizes the questions as open- or closed-ended by recording an O or C near each one. Refer to page 70 if the group needs to review this idea. At the end, brainstorm a few more open-ended questions that you could add to the list.

Discussion format: Six Hats Thinking (20 minutes)

1. High-Five Partners (same as sharing partners) count off using the six types of quality questions from Appendix F, page 271: Knowledge, Comprehension, Application, Analysis, Synthesis, and Evaluation Questions. The first pair says, "knowledge," the second says, "comprehension," etc.

2. Choose a new sharing topic from the list generated at the first meeting and ask for a volunteer to share about the chosen topic.

3. Allow partners one minute to generate a question for the sharer that fits their assigned type of question.

4. Each pair asks a question of the sharer.

5. Reassign question categories by counting off partners again; each pair will have a new type of question.

6. Repeat steps 3-6 as time allows, reassigning types of questions after each share.

Reflect: Whole group (5-10 minutes)

Call attention to how sharing skills have been gradually developed in the meetings so far: *In the sharing portion of our meetings, how have we gradually developed, task by task, the skills needed for quality conversation?*

Record responses on a chart. If necessary, remind participants of sharing skills explored:

- **Meeting One:** Sticky Note Share, suggested sharing topics

- **Meeting Two:** Whip Share, using one of the topics from the first meeting

- **Meeting Three:** no share; we created a list of questions for Whip Share topic from the second meeting

- **Meeting Four:** Partner Share; we further explored Whip Share using the questions generated at the third meeting; explored new sharing topics from list using different types of questions

What might we be ready for next? What sharing exercise would continue to develop student discussion skills?

Suggested additional sharing formats:

- Individual share with the whole group asking questions from the six categories of questions

- Individual share followed by practice making supportive comments

- Extend individual share to one minute (prompting more extemporaneous sharing), followed by questions and comments

- Extend individual share up to three minutes, followed by questions and comments

Prepare for the next meeting

Announce next meeting date. Direct participants to Meeting Five's introduction and Reading Assignment, pages 36-37 in this *Study Guide,* to prepare for the next meeting. Acknowledge the volunteer(s) named on the daily news chart for offering to tabulate the chart data and report at Meeting Eight.

Follow-up

Discuss and select from these follow-up possibilities.

- Try a Whip Share with your students or at a staff meeting.

- Continue sharing with your students, incrementally moving toward give-and-take conversations.

NOTES

The Circle of Power and Respect, Activity

PARTICIPANT INSTRUCTIONS

Chapter Two provides detailed information about the activity component of the Circle of Power and Respect. The purpose of an activity is to help students build relationships, develop academic and social skills, and have fun with each other. Appendix D describes many activities developmentally suited to adolescents.

Keep in mind

Activities vary widely in complexity and risk. Teachers need to assess the skills of a group in order to plan an activity that will be appropriate and successful. Readiness is the key to successful activities.

Discussion format at a glance: Shake It Up

Shake It Up is a chair-changing game that can be used to share or review information. Everyone is seated in a circle, and the leader reads statements that prompt participants to either change chairs or remain seated.

Reading Assignment

In Chapter Two, read the Activity section, pages 74-83. Skim Appendix D, pages 235-264, to get ideas for CPR activities.

Interact with the text: Connection to Self

Consider the questions: What are four ways that you try to meet the adolescent need for fun in your classroom? How do students respond? As you skim Appendix D, pages 235-264, star at least five activities that you are interested in exploring at the next meeting.

What are four ways that you try to meet the adolescent need for fun in your classroom? How do students respond?

1.

2.

3.

4.

LEADER INSTRUCTIONS

Meeting Preparation

Familiarize yourself with the meeting formats, including the greeting, sharing, and Shake It Up formats. Plan how you will create pairs or triads for the activity.

Materials: Materials for daily news chart

Daily news

Prepare and post daily news chart: As before, the poll on this chart will be analyzed and results reported at Meeting Eight.

Date: _____

Good Afternoon, Movers!

Welcome to meeting five of our study group. Today we will discuss how to use activities to meet students' need for fun and develop social and academic competencies at the same time.

Do you play cooperative games with students? (Make a tally mark)

Never   Rarely   Sometimes   Often   Always

Let's get moving!

(sign)

Data tabulation volunteer(s):

Meeting

Gather in a circle

Post and refer to the rules

Ask a participant to read the rules. Group members choose a rule to pay special attention to during the meeting.

Follow-up from last meeting (5 minutes)

Ask participants to share follow-up experiences (see *Guide* page 35).

Introduce topic

Today we'll play a lively game as an example of the activities we can use in CPR. We will discuss some important considerations for teachers when choosing an activity.

Guide greeting, sharing, and Shake It Up discussion format

Greet: Elevator Greeting (5 minutes)

Participants stand close together facing the same direction, as if in a crowded elevator. Each person greets and is greeted by two or three of the people closest to him/her, (*Good Morning, _____*), while everyone keeps looking at an imaginary floor indicator above the imaginary elevator door. Challenge participants to make the greeting friendly even though they are not looking at one another.

Share: Individual Share with comments (10 minutes)

Choose a new sharing topic from the list generated at the first meeting. Have one or two participants share about the topic and then invite questions and comments. Encourage the group to ask open-ended questions (refer to Appendix F, page 271 if necessary).

Introduction to making comments

Today we'll choose a new sharing topic from our list, and we will add another dimension to our conversation: we will ask listeners to make comments as well as ask questions.

Review the purposes and types of comments (pages 71-72):

- closing comments (these close the conversation and acknowledge the sharer)
- comments that make connections
- boomerang comments (these end with a question to the sharer)

Comment examples

Joe, it sounds as if you are looking forward to your trip. I hope you have a great time. Thanks for sharing. (closing comment)

I went hiking at that park, too, and I thought the waterfall was the best part! How did you like the waterfall? (connection and boomerang comment)

Discussion format: Shake It Up (20 minutes)

1. Preparation to play: *To prepare for today's study, choose one activity and learn a few details about why and how to play the game.*

Create pairs or triads and ask participants to choose an activity from Appendix D (pages 235-264).

Participants may refer to the activities they starred before the meeting. Allow five minutes for the partners to clarify the rules of the game and discuss how they would use that activity with their students. Have each pair think about the logistics of the activity (in a circle, standing, etc.) and the purpose of the activity.

2. Form a circle with enough room in the middle for people to get up and move among the chairs.

3. Explain the rules of Shake It Up: *I will read you a general statement about activities. Think about whether or not it applies to the activity that you chose; move to a different chair if it does, and stay seated if it doesn't. For example, if I say "This activity is done in partnerships" and your activity is done in partnerships, you move to a different—unoccupied!—chair in the circle. If your activity is not done in partnerships, you remain seated for this round.*

Statements for Shake It Up:
This activity is best for when students are just becoming acquainted with each other.
This activity helps students develop observation skills.
This activity requires students to agree on a topic, idea, or theme.
This activity helps students learn academic content.
This activity helps students build trust with each other.
This activity involves lots of movement.
This activity involves elimination.
This activity helps students learn new information about each other.
This activity requires students to take social risks.
This activity provides opportunities for students to acknowledge each other.
This activity usually creates a lot of laughter.

4. Model how to quickly and safely change chairs (refer to page 78).

5. Play the game. After each round of chair-changing, have some participants who changed chairs name and describe their activity and how it fits the statement. For example, if the statement referred to activities that are good for building relationships, the partners who had such an activity could briefly describe the activity and how it fosters student relationship building.

Reflect: Individual written response (5 minutes)

Ask participants to respond to the following questions in the Notes section.
What insights did you gain from hearing about various activities and how they can be used in the classroom?

Write down the names of two activities you might try with your students.

Prepare for the next meeting

Announce next meeting date. Direct participants to Meeting Six's introduction and Reading Assignment, pages 42-43 in this *Study Guide*, to prepare for the next meeting. Acknowledge the volunteer(s) named on the daily news chart for offering to tabulate the chart data and report at Meeting Eight.

Optional: If you have not already viewed the student-led CPR portions of *The Circle of Power and Respect Advisory Meeting* DVD, you may choose to view it before or during Meeting Six.

Follow-up

Discuss and select from these follow-up possibilities.

- Try leading an activity during your advisory time and/or during a class period. Before the next meeting, set a time to meet and check in with each other to share experiences of leading new activities. Help each other problem solve any difficulties.

- Lead an activity at the next staff meeting.

The Circle of Power and Respect, Daily News Processing and Student-led CPR

PARTICIPANT INSTRUCTIONS

The final two sections of Chapter Two provide information about processing a daily news message and the rationale and preparation for student-led Circle of Power and Respect meetings.

Keep in mind

One premise of *The Advisory Book* is that CPR nurtures responsible independence in adolescents through meeting their needs for relationship, autonomy, competence, and fun. Full participation in a CPR satisfies student needs, but responsible independence is most robustly developed when they lead all or part of the meeting themselves.

Discussion format at a glance: Talking Cards

On an index card, participants respond to a question or comment on a topic. Working in small groups, participants shuffle, discuss, and sort the cards so that each opinion is heard anonymously. This way, the cards "do the talking."

Reading Assignment

In Chapter Two, read the Daily News and Student-led CPR sections, pages 83-97.

Interact with the text

Find daily news examples: As you read through the Daily News section (pages 83-89), to help you understand why the daily news is an important element in community-building, write down specific examples of how daily news serves the purposes stated at the beginning of the section (top of page 83).

Message Purpose: to inform the community about the day and/or the advisory
Examples
1. *Teacher writes a sidebar that reminds and/or the advisory students that it is picture day*
_____
2.
_____

3.
_____

Message Purpose: to ease the transition into the day
Examples
1. *Interactive question asks students to check in on their mood that morning*
_____
2.
_____

3.
_____

Message Purpose: to practice social and academic skills
Examples
1. *Students write an example of a balanced equation to review a math concept*
_____
2.
_____

3.
_____

Consider student-led CPR: As you read through the student-led CPR section (pages 89-97), to help you evaluate the importance of letting students lead CPR, list benefits and challenges of student-led CPRs for both the student and the teacher.

Benefits of Student-led CPR	Challenges of Student-led CPR

LEADER INSTRUCTIONS

Meeting Preparation

Familiarize yourself with the meeting format, including the greeting, sharing, and Talking Cards formats. Decide how you will divide into groups of four or five people each. Determine if you will show the student-led meeting portions of *The Circle of Power and Respect Advisory Meeting* DVD during this meeting. Even if the group has already watched the recording, reviewing this portion could be a helpful reminder. After you introduce the topic or in a separate session outside of this meeting are both good opportunities to watch.

Materials: Materials for daily news chart; index cards; sharing topic list from the first meeting; (optional) *The Circle of Power and Respect Advisory Meeting* DVD and DVD player

Daily news

Prepare and post daily news chart: As before, the poll on this chart will be analyzed and results reported at Meeting Eight.

Date: _____

Good afternoon,

Welcome to our sixth book-study meeting. At today's session we will discuss the benefits and challenges of student-led CPRs.

Is it important to intentionally help students transition into the school day? (Make a tally mark)

Not important   Somewhat important   Important

DO NOW: On 2 separate index cards, write 1 benefit and 1 challenge associated with student-led CPRs (one item per index card, no signature).

Sincerely,

(sign)

Meeting

Gather in a circle

Post and refer to the rules

Ask a participant to read the rules. Each member assesses how she or he feels the group has been doing so far with the group guidelines by showing one, two, three, four, or five fingers (five is the most positive evaluation). Allow a few minutes to discuss and record any ideas for improvement that the group agrees upon.

Follow-up from last meeting (5 minutes)

Ask participants to share follow-up experiences (see *Guide* page 41).

Introduce topic

So far in our book study, we have focused on how teachers can best facilitate CPR meetings with students. While reading this chapter, you noted ways that daily news fulfills its purposes. Today we'll focus on the second part of the chapter—student-led CPRs. We'll have a lively discussion about their benefits and challenges.

Optional: View the student-led CPR portions of *The Circle of Power of Respect Advisory Meeting* DVD.

Guide greeting, sharing, and Talking Cards discussion format

Greet: Silent Greeting (2 minutes)

The challenge with this greeting is to show friendliness without saying anything. One person at a time greets the person to her right without using words or other sounds and is greeted back silently with the same or a different gesture. The greeting continues around the circle until all have been greeted.

Share: Individual Share with reflection (5-7 minutes)

Allow time for one or two participants to share. The sharer chooses a topic from the list generated at the first meeting. The audience responds with questions and comments. At the end of each share, ask the sharer: How important was it to choose the topic yourself?

Discussion format: Talking Cards (20 minutes)

1. Divide into groups of four or five people each.

2. Participants place their index cards from the daily news DO NOW assignment in the center of their group. All cards are shuffled together.

3. One at a time, group members pull cards at random and read them aloud; the group comments on the benefits and discusses

strategies for addressing the challenges of student-led CPRs as expressed on the cards. Like cards can be grouped together. Remind participants to refer back to the book during their discussion for information about challenges and benefits of student-led CPRs.

Reflect: Whole group and individual (10-12 minutes)

Whole group: Each group shares with the whole group a challenge from their Talking Cards and the strategies they discussed to meet the challenge. The leader scribes challenges and strategies on a T-chart (see example below).

Challenges	Strategies

Individual: Ask participants to answer the following question in the Notes.

What do you think are benefits of student-led CPRs for the teacher and students?

Prepare for the next meeting

Announce next meeting date. Direct participants to Meeting Seven's introduction and Reading Assignment, pages 48-49 in this *Study Guide,* to prepare for the next meeting. Acknowledge the volunteer(s) named on the daily news chart for offering to tabulate the chart data and report at Meeting Eight.

Follow-up

Discuss and select from these follow-up possibilities. If the group decides to work collaboratively, designate a leader.

- Initiate student-led meetings.

- Teams meet to plan daily news charts together.

NOTES

MEETING SEVEN

Activity Plus Advisories

PARTICIPANT INSTRUCTIONS

Chapter Three introduces a second format for advisory: Activity Plus (A+). This structure provides more time for the activity than the time allowed for the activity in a CPR meeting. The A+ format consists of four components: daily news, greeting, activity, and reflection.

Keep in mind

In addition to advisory, many teachers follow the A+ format for their content classes throughout the day.

Discussion format at a glance: Sample Activity Plus meeting

This meeting follows the format of an Activity Plus advisory: daily news, greeting, activity, and reflection.

Reading Assignment

Read Chapter Three: Activity Plus (A+) Advisories, pages 99-102; Skim pages 103-122 to see various examples of A+ meetings.

Interact with the text: Venn diagram comparison of CPR and A+

Read about the Activity Plus format on pages 101-105, and create a Venn diagram to compare and contrast the two types of advisory formats, CPR and A+. Look through the examples of A+ meetings described on pages 103-122. Note two meetings that you are interested in trying with your students.

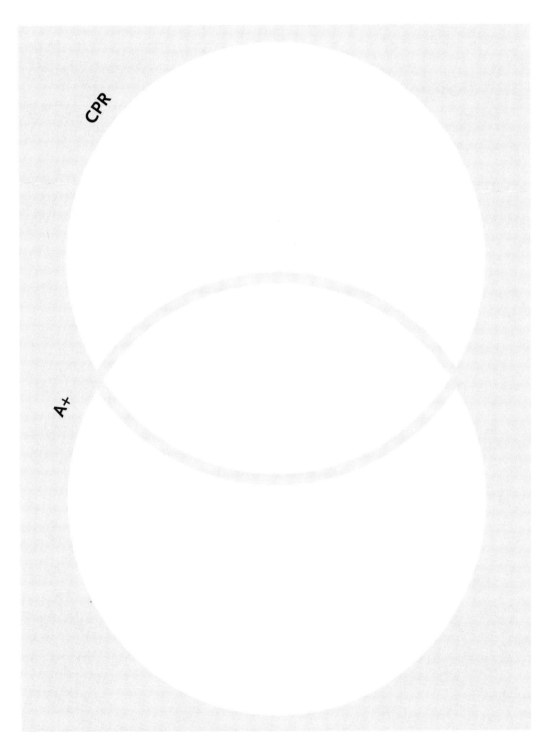

LEADER INSTRUCTIONS

Meeting Preparation

Familiarize yourself with the Activity Plus meeting format.

Materials: Materials for daily news chart; a popsicle stick for each participant with his/her name on it (for drawing names)

Daily news

Prepare and post daily news chart: As before, the poll on this chart will be analyzed and the results reported at Meeting Eight.

Date: _____

Greetings!

Today's session will focus on the Activity Plus (A+) advisory meeting. We'll explore how to use this format not only during our advisory time, but throughout the day.

Let's check in to see how CPR is coming along in our advisories. Are you implementing the four components of CPR? Put a tally next to each component that you are using:

GREETING   SHARING   ACTIVITY   DAILY NEWS

DO NOW: Review the sample A+ meetings on pages 103-122. Find a partner, and together sign up for an A+ that you will present to the group together. You will have a little time to prepare your presentation during the meeting.

Write your names and the name of your sample A+ below:

Thanks for your participation!

(sign)

Data tabulation volunteer(s):

Meeting

Gather in a circle

Post and refer to rules (2 minutes)

Choose one of the rules and ask for a volunteer from the group to be a process observer at today's meeting. The process observer participates in the meeting with the additional role of looking for examples of ways the group observed or failed the rule. The process observer reports at the end of the meeting.

Follow-up from last meeting (5 minutes)

Ask participants to share follow-up experiences (see *Guide* page 46).

Introduce topic

Today we will explore an advisory structure that is different from CPR. The A+ format was designed for those times when the activity you want to do takes more time than the approximately five minutes allotted to the activity in CPR. In A+ you have about 15 minutes for a more extended activity. To get the feel of this format, we'll review some sample A+ meetings.

Guide sample Activity Plus format

Daily news (3 minutes)

Allow a few minutes for participants to find a partner and sign up for today's activity.

Greeting: Shape Greeting (3 minutes)

Turning to the person on her left, one person makes a shape with her hands; her partner completes the shape by making the other side of the shape. Example: *Good morning, Al* (makes a v-shape with fingers). *Good morning, Nicole* (makes an upside-down v-shape with his fingers and connects his fingertips to hers, creating a diamond shape).

Discussion format: Prepare and describe a sample A+ meeting (25 minutes)

1. Prepare: Allow ten minutes for each pair to prepare a presentation for the whole group on their chosen sample A+. Partners should be sure they understand their sample meeting and brainstorm when and for what purpose teachers could use this A+ meeting. For example, using the Team-building A+ (page 111), teachers might use the meeting mid-winter when students are getting restless for more vigorous activities.

2. Describe: Each pair presents a sample A+. Allow no more than two minutes for each presentation (15 minutes total). Draw name sticks to determine the order of presentations. Each presentation

should include a meeting summary and how they would use the meeting with their students. You may not have time for everyone to present.

Reflect: Whole group (10 minutes)

Which of the sample A+ meetings presented can you envision using regularly? Consider whether you could use some of the formats school-wide or consistently across grades or teams.

How could the A+ meeting be used to structure a class period? (E.g., In a math class, begin with a Skip Greeting, teach the lesson and have students practice a variety of ways to solve word problems (activity), and close with a reflection on the advantage of knowing how to solve a problem in multiple ways.)

Process observer

Ask the process observer to report to the group on how well the group followed the selected rule.

Prepare for the next meeting

Announce next meeting date. Direct participants to Meeting Eight's introduction and Reading Assignment, pages 54-55 in this *Study Guide*, to prepare for the next meeting. Acknowledge the volunteer named on the daily news chart for offering to tabulate the chart data. Remind all tabulation volunteers that they will report on their tabulations at the next meeting.

Follow-up

Discuss and select from these follow-up possibilities. If the group decides to work collaboratively, designate a leader.

- Try an A+ meeting in advisory or a class period.

- If participants envision using A+ meetings across teams or grades, schedule a follow-up meeting for further planning for this implementation.

- Set a time to meet and check in with each other before the next meeting to share how your A+ meeting trial went. Help each other problem solve any difficulties.

NOTES

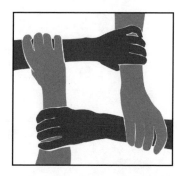

Planning Advisories

PARTICIPANT INSTRUCTIONS

Chapter Four describes ways for teachers to individually or collaboratively plan advisory meetings. This chapter helps teachers plan using the provided thematic advisories or to create their own advisories using the vast activity, greeting, and sharing resources in the book. Guidance is also provided for choosing the meeting format and challenge level.

Keep in mind

The book suggests using the repeatable formats of CPR and A+ for planning advisories. See the sample advisories provided in the chapter for academically- and personally-focused content and for the "pick-and-choose" approach. See Appendix A for a full listing of greeting, share, and activity descriptions with challenge level and other qualities noted.

Discussion format at a glance: Planning Workshop

Participants will use a guide to help plan advisory meetings.

Reading Assignment

Read Chapter Four: Planning Advisories, pages 125-131; skim Appendix A: Greeting, Share, and Activity Index, pages 211-215. Review the Advisory Planning Guide below. Be prepared to decide what period of time you are planning for, whether you will plan individually or as a team, and what planning approaches you will use.

Prepare for data sharing: If you tabulated the data from one of the daily news charts, you will share the findings at today's meeting.

Interact with the text: Summarize and Apply

As you read through this chapter, make a list of items to keep in mind when planning advisories.

1.

2.

3.

4.

5.

Advisory Planning Guide

Time period covered? (week, month, semester, year)

Individual or team planning? If in teams, how will teams share responsibility?

Approach?
- Thematic (invented or selected from Thematic Units, pages 139-207)
- Academic focus (math, language arts, science, social studies-- see page 126-127 example)
- Personal focus (weekend news/plans, preference/opinion polls--see page 127 example)
- Teacher/student choices (invented or selected from appendices of greetings, shares, and activities)

LEADER INSTRUCTIONS

Meeting Preparation

Familiarize yourself with the meeting formats, including the greeting, sharing, and Planning Workshop formats.

Materials: Materials for the daily news chart

Daily news

Prepare and post daily news chart

Date: _____

Greetings, Friends!

We have looked deeply at CPR and had lively discussions about this structure. Today we will focus on planning for implementation of both CPR and A+ in our school.

We will also look at the data that we have been collecting in each meeting's daily news chart.

Warmly,

(sign)

Meeting

Gather in a circle

Post and refer to the rules

Ask for a volunteer to read the rules aloud. Ask participants to think about all of the book-study meetings. In partners, have participants share about a rule that was followed consistently throughout the sessions and provide evidence to support their thinking.

Follow-up from last meeting (5 minutes)

Ask participants to share follow-up experiences (see *Guide* page 52).

Introduce topic

Chapter Four of The Advisory Book *has many teacher resources for planning CPR and A+ meetings. Today we'll explore those resources and apply them in our planning workshop.*

Guide greeting, sharing, and Planning Workshop discussion format

Greet: Basic Greeting (2 minutes)

Share: Data sharing (10 minutes)

Individuals or partners take turns presenting data findings from daily news chart questions. Allow one or two questions and comments from the group after each presentation. Acknowledge the additional work and contributions made by the data tabulation volunteers.

Discussion format: Planning Workshop (25 minutes)

1. Quick Partner Share: Share one item from your list to keep in mind when planning advisory meetings.

2. Review the Advisory Planning Guide on page 55 in this *Study Guide*. Individuals, teams, or the whole group select a planning time frame and approach(es).

3. Planning time. Participants may work alone or with colleagues, recording their planning in the Notes or on a separate piece of paper. (20 minutes)

Reflect: Whole group (5 minutes)

Ask each group or individual to share an outcome from their planning workshop with the whole group: *What will help you continue to use CPR and A+ advisory structures with your students?*

Prepare for the next meeting

Announce next meeting date. Direct participants to Meeting Nine's introduction and Reading Assignment, pages 60-61 in this *Study Guide,* to prepare for the next meeting.

Follow-up

Discuss and select from these follow-up possibilities. If the group decides to work collaboratively, designate a leader.

- Schedule team or staff meetings that might be needed to further implement advisory meetings in your school.

- Meet regularly to check in with each other regarding the plans made at this meeting for implementation of the advisory structures.

NOTES

Assessing Social Skill Development

PARTICIPANT INSTRUCTIONS

Advisory is a powerful context for taking on challenging social issues such as bullying and multicultural understanding. However, the students need to be ready to talk about such topics safely and respectfully. In this meeting, you will gain tools for assessing and boosting the social skills of your students so they can address challenging social issues. The degree to which students generally demonstrate social skills during CPR and Advisory Plus can serve as an indicator of their readiness to talk about social issues.

In this final meeting, you will apply a Social Skills in CPR Assessment Tool to measure the social proficiencies of your advisory groups. You will consider the results, and then identify support in *The Advisory Book* for strengthening the social skills of your students.

Meeting format at a glance: Sample A+

This meeting follows the format of an A+ Advisory: daily news, greeting, activity, and reflection.

Reading Assignment

1. Read Appendix E: Assessing Social Skills, pages 267-269. Use the Social Skills in CPR Assessment Tool on page 268 to evaluate the degree to which your advisory students demonstrate the skills necessary for challenging conversations on social topics.

2. Identify social skills that are especially weak in your group, then review *The Advisory Book,* Chapter Two, for advice on addressing those issues. See text interaction below.

Interact with the text: Ways to build student social skills in CPR

Review *The Advisory Book,* Chapter Two, pages 31-88, to find tips on boosting specific social skills in CPR components. Use the table below to record social weaknesses you've noticed in your students, and note the book's advice on how to address the problem.

The Advisory Book **Support for Social Skill Development**

WEAKNESS	SUGGESTIONS FOR ADDRESSING WEAKNESS
Example: poor eye contact during greeting	Pages 52-53, maintain rigor over general tone of greeting
Example: low self-control during activity/game	Page 82, choose challenge level appropriate to students' self-control

LEADER INSTRUCTIONS

Meeting Preparation

Decide how you will divide group into four small groups.

Materials: Materials for the daily news chart

Daily news

Prepare and post daily news chart

Date: _____

Hello, Fine Colleagues,

Welcome to the last session of our book study. In preparation for this meeting,

1. We used the Social Skills in CPR Assessment Tool to determine the degree to which our students demonstrate good social skills in advisory.

2. We looked for ways we can use <u>The Advisory Book</u> as a resource to further strengthen social skills..

Indicate below with a check mark the CPR component in which your students showed the highest level of social skills.

Greeting   Sharing   Activity   Daily News

I look forward to reflecting together,

(sign)

Meeting

Gather in a circle

Post and refer to rules

Follow-up from last meeting (5 minutes)

Ask participants to share follow-up experiences (see *Guide* page 58).

Introduce topic

We've worked together for eight sessions to explore the advisory structure as a way to build the relationships and social skills that strengthen community. A supportive community can counterbalance negative tendencies. As we help students develop social skills, we help create a healthy climate in our school. Today we'll discuss what we found when we assessed our students' social skills in CPR, how The Advisory Book *can help us address weaknesses, and how ready our students are for advisory conversations on challenging social topics, such as bullying. Please have the charts from the assignment ready.*

Guide sample A+ meeting format

Greeting: Left-Right Greeting (1 minute)

Participants greet the people to their right and left in the circle by saying, *Good afternoon, _____.*

Activity: Reviewing assessment of and book support for social skill development (30 minutes)

1. Divide into groups of four.

2. Group members have in hand the two assigned charts:
   Social Skills in CPR Assessment
   The Advisory Book Support for Social Skill Development

3. Group members take turns sharing their assessment results with the group. Each describes a strength, a weakness, and one piece of advice from *The Advisory Book* to address the weakness, then invites the others to add any suggestions they can think of, based on the book. As people share, group members may record ideas on their book support charts.

Activity: Partner and whole-group discussion: Use of advisories to address social issues (10 minutes)

Do you think your current advisory group is ready to respectfully and productively tackle a challenging social issue? Give evidence that supports your assessment.

Allow participants a few minutes to reflect. Partners share their assessments and evidence. Invite volunteers to share out with the whole group.

Reflect: Individual and whole group (5 minutes)

Individual written response in the Notes section:

1. *How have your social skills affected your life?*

2. *Refer back to your study group goal recorded in the Notes section of Meeting One. To what degree did you reach your goal? How did the group help you reach your goal?*

Whole group: Ask for volunteers to share about how the group helped them reach their goals.

Follow-up

Discuss how the Social Skills in CPR Assessment Tool can help you reflect on the social-emotional growth of an advisory group throughout the year.

- Assess social skills for each component of a particular CPR in the fall, mid-year, and near the end of the year.

- Invite your students to assess with you, appealing to their desire for autonomy by having them self-assess the degree to which their group is maturing socially.

- When students are ready, implement advisory themes to address bullying or multicultural understanding or other sensitive issues. See *The Advisory Book* for sample advisories on these topics (Unit Four: Multicultural Understanding, pages 184-195, and Unit Six: Witnessing Bullying, pages 202-205).

NOTES

Discussion and Group Formats

DISCUSSION FORMATS

Affinity Process

In Affinity Process, small groups meet to discuss a topic or respond to a discussion question. Then groups combine to create a larger group, share their previous discussions, and combine their ideas into a new collective response. This process of combining groups continues until participants are in one large group with one consolidated idea.

Inside-Outside Circle

Participants form a circle within a circle and pair up to discuss a reading question. After each paired discussion, the inside circle moves clockwise a set number of spaces (e.g., two spaces) to talk with a new outside-circle person about the same question or a new question.

Six Hats Thinking

In groups of six, members assume one of six distinct viewpoints, or one "hat." (If there are more than six people per group, two people can represent one hat.) The six points of view are provided by the leader and are relevant to the text read. Each person briefly describes his point of view to the group. For example, the group leader asks a question, and each hat/person says how it would respond to that situation. Finally, the group can choose to decide which response(s) would be best.

Talking Cards

On an index card, participants respond to a question or comment on a topic. Working in small groups, participants shuffle and discuss the cards so that each opinion is heard anonymously. In this way, the cards do the talking. When there are many cards per group, cards can be sorted and those with similar content can be grouped together for discussion.

Shake it Up

Create a circle of chairs with one less chair than there are students. Students sit in chairs, except for one who stands in the center. Each player is given a card with the name of something that fits into the designated category, such as elements in the periodic table. The student in the center makes a statement related to the category beginning with, *Shake it up if....* For example, a student could say, *Shake it up if your element is a gas.* The players whose cards match the statement try to find a new chair to sit in. The student who made the statement also tries to find a seat. Whoever doesn't find a seat is the caller in the center. She repeats the process by making a new statement about the category. Allow time after each change of chairs for students to discuss why they did or didn't shake it up.

VARIATION

Play this game without the caller in the center of the circle. Instead, the teacher or leader can read from a list of prepared statements.

PARTNER AND SMALL GROUPS FORMATION

Count Off

Students count off by a designated number depending on the number of groups necessary for the activity. For example, if six groups are needed, students count off by sixes. For variation, students can count off in different languages, or use the same method and name seasons or compass directions.

Screaming Eyes

Students stand in a circle with their eyes looking at the floor. At the count of three, they lift their eyes and scream if they make contact with another pair or eyes. Those who make eye contact are then partners. Repeat until everyone has a partner.

High Five Partners

Starting at one end of a circle or row, one student begins by turning in the designated direction (right or left) and giving the person next to her a high-five. After the first partnership is identified, the process continues with the next student until everyone has a partner.

Categories

Students group themselves according to how they fit into a particular category, such as pet ownership or place of birth. The teacher or a volunteer designates the category. After the category is announced, students work as a group using verbal or non-verbal signals to appropriately group themselves. For example, if the category is pet ownership, students may identify the type(s) of pets they own with gestures and find others in the groups to form a group (cat owners find other cat owners, dog and cat owners find other dog and cat owners). If a certain number is required for the activity and groups are too large, challenge the groups to subdivide using a subcategory. For example, a large group of dog owners could split into two groups according to the size or breed of their dogs.

Card Groups

Alter a deck of cards to match the type of grouping that you need for an activity. For example, if you need four groups of five, you can alter the deck to make sure that you have five cards for each of the suits. Distribute one card to each student and allow them a few minutes to mingle and find their group members.

ORIGINS DEVELOPMENTAL DESIGNS®

Helping Adolescents Succeed in School

This book was developed through the work of Origins, a nonprofit educational organization and creator of the *Developmental Designs*™ approach. The approach consists of highly practical strategies designed to integrate social and academic learning for adolescents, increasing motivation and self-management, and strengthening connections to school.

Developmental Designs Teaching Practices

Advisory—The Circle of Power and Respect (CPR) and Activity Plus (A+) meeting structures build community, social skills, and readiness for learning.

Goal Setting—Students declare a personal stake in school to anchor their learning in a meaningful commitment to growth.

Social Contract—Based on their personal goals, students design and sign an agreement that binds the community to common rules.

Modeling and Practicing—Nothing is assumed; all routines are practiced. Social competencies are learned by seeing and doing.

The Loop—Ongoing, varied reflective planning and assessments ensure continuous, conscious growth.

Empowering Language—Gesture, voice, and words combine to create a rigorous, respectful climate for building responsible independence.

Pathways to Self-control—When rules are broken, teachers have an array of strategies, such as redirections, loss of privilege, and take a break. Self-management grows without loss of dignity.

Problem-solving Strategies—Students and teachers use social conferencing, problem-solving meetings, and other structures to find positive solutions to chronic problems.

Practices for Motivating Instruction—Student choice, bridging, structured interaction, and other practices help connect young adolescent needs and the school curriculum, so that students are deeply engaged in learning.

Power of Play—Play is designed to build community, enliven students, and restore their focus, ensuring more time on task.

Learn more about the *Developmental Designs* approach through:

Professional Development Opportunities

- One-day and week-long workshops for middle-level educators
- Classroom coaching to support implementation
- School-wide consultation providing training and support for sustainability

Publications and Resources

- Books, DVDs, and study guides for middle-level educators
- Free newsletter supporting beginning and experienced *Developmental Designs* practitioners
- Web site with hundreds of free advisory and lesson resources: www.developmentaldesigns.org

For details, contact:

米ORIGINS

3805 Grand Avenue South
Minneapolis, Minnesota 55409
612-822-3422 • 800-543-8715 • Fax: 612-822-3585
www.developmentaldesigns.org

More *Developmental Designs* Publications

*Classroom Discipline:
Guiding Adolescents to
Responsible Independence*
Origins, 2009, 304 pages

*Classroom Discipline
Study Guide*
Origins, 2012, 84 pages

*Tried and True Classroom
Games and Greetings:
Grades 4–9*
Origins, 2010, 76 pages

*The Circle of Power and Respect
Advisory Meeting* (DVD)
Origins, 2011, 70 minutes, viewing
guide included

*Modeling and Practicing
Classroom Routines* DVD
Origins, 2012, 38 minutes, viewing
guide included